WHEN YOU'VE DONE YOUR BEST

Written & Illustrated
by
Marcia A. Neese

Edited by
Marjorie L. Oelerich, Ph.D.
Professor of Early Childhood & Elementary
Education, Mankato State University
&
John Cranfill, M.S.
Coordinator of Child and Adolescent Service,
Davis Psychiatry Clinic, Indianapolis, Indiana

BSP

BAKER STREET PRODUCTIONS, LTD.
Mankato, Minnesota, U.S.A.

Library of Congress Cataloging in Publication Data

Neese, Marcia A.
When you've done your best.

(The Boulder Gang)
Summary: After receiving a low grade for refusing to dissect a frog, Tina tries to hide her report card from her mother but finally learns that she can't be perfect at everything.
[1. Success—Fiction. 2. Honesty—Fiction. 3. Schools—Fiction]
I. Oelerich, Marjorie L. II. Title. III. Series: Neese, Marcia A. Boulder Gang.
PZ7.N385Wh 1984 [E] 83-22424
ISBN 0-914867-03-2

BAKER STREET PRODUCTIONS, LTD.
839 Belgrade Avenue, Box 3610, Mankato, MN 56002-3610

WHEN YOU'VE DONE YOUR BEST

Sometimes it's hard when you've done your best, but you feel that your best just isn't good enough. At least, Tina Tansell thought so.

Tina Tansell was a very good student. She always made straight A's on her report card. Tina loved Math and Reading. She was also very good at Spelling and Geography. But Tina had a brand new subject this year. The subject was Science. This semester they were studying and dissecting insects and other animals.

Tina hated Science class. All those insects, worms and frogs. "Yuk!" thought Tina. "How can the teacher make us cut up these things? I just can't do it!"

Tina didn't mind reading her Science book and taking the written tests, but those things were only a part of the grade. Dissecting counted for most of the grade on the final report card.

Because Andy Andrews and Sherry Summers were younger, they were not in the Science class. The rest of the Gang, except Tina, were doing fine with dissecting. Billy Boulder wanted to be a veterinarian when he grew up, so he was making straight A's in this part of the class. Becky Boulder was doing pretty well, too. Timmy Thomas and Mikie Murphy were doing okay, even though they did fool around in class and put pieces of worms in their pockets to scare the other kids. Jessica Jones wasn't having problems, and even Patty Peterson was doing better than anyone ever thought she would. Only Tina was having trouble.

Tina was really worried about the grade she was going to get at the end of the semester.

One day after school, Tina found Andy and Sherry playing in Sherry's sandbox. "I don't know what I'm going to do," Tina said to them. "I know I'm not going to make a good grade in Science. My mom is going to be so mad at me when I get my report card."

"What's the problem?" asked Andy. "You're a good student. You always make straight A's."

"I know, Andy," said Tina. "I do really well on all my other subjects, but I just can't get Science. I can't stand to cut up those insects and frogs."

"Cut them up?" screeched Andy. "You mean you have to cut up live bugs and things?"

"No, they aren't alive, Andy," said Tina. "But we do have to dissect them. The teacher says it's the best way to learn about them and how their hearts and stomachs work.

"Everyone else is doing fine in class," continued Tina. "I'm the only one who can't seem to be able to cut into those animals. I'm afraid I will hurt them. I know they can't feel anything, but I just can't do it!"

"Have you talked to the teacher about it?" asked Sherry Summers. "Maybe he won't make you cut them up. Maybe he won't give you a bad grade after all."

"I did talk to him," said Tina. "He says I have to do the dissecting if I want to make an A in Science."

"So, making A's isn't everything," said Sherry Summers.

"It is to my mom," sighed Tina. "Mom is always so proud of me when I bring home all A's. I'm afraid she'll be mad at me if I don't make an A."

"Well, you better do something," said Andy. "We get our report cards in just two weeks."

"I know," cried Tina. "I just don't know what I'm going to do."

Tina was so upset when she got home that she couldn't even eat dinner.

"Aren't you feeling well?" asked Tina's mom. "You haven't eaten a bite."

"Oh, I'm feeling fine, Mom," said Tina. "I'm just not very hungry."

Tina helped her mom do the dishes after dinner. "I think I'll go to my room and study my Science," said Tina.

Tina went into her room and stretched out across her bed with her book. She started reading the chapter on frogs. Billy Boulder had reminded her that they were going to dissect some frogs in class the following week.

As Tina read, her eyelids got heavier and heavier. Finally, they were so heavy that she couldn't keep them open. She was thinking about cutting up frogs in Science class the following week.

All of a sudden, Tina seemed to be floating way up in the clear blue sky. She was floating over a beautiful green meadow. The tall grasses were bending in the breeze. The smell of clover in full bloom filled the air. Then she was gliding on a soft breeze over the houses and yards of her neighborhood.

The breeze carried Tina to a quiet little pond, where it gently set her down on the shore beside a patch of cattails and lily pads. She sat there just watching as the breeze made tiny ripples on the surface of the pond. Then, in the blink of an eye, a big green frog jumped out of the water and onto a lily pad next to Tina. It was wearing a silky blue top hat and a red bow tie. It had a shiny gold badge on its chest.

"Hello . . . ribbit . . . my name is Stanley Froghorn," he said. "Who are you and what do you want here?"

"Hello, Mr. Froghorn," replied Tina. "I'm not quite sure what I'm doing here or even how I got here. I'm not even sure where this place is. My name is Tina Tansell."

"You must know . . . ribbit . . . how you got here," said Stanley Froghorn. "Otherwise, you wouldn't be here."

"Well, I was studying dissecting frogs in my Science book when . . . ," Tina started to explain, but Stanley Froghorn rudely interrupted her.

"Dissecting!" he exclaimed. "Now I understand! You want to catch me . . . ribbit . . . and my family and cut us up into little pieces . . . ribbit . . . just so you can see what made us live!"

"Oh, no!" cried Tina. "I don't want to do that! In fact, I'm making bad grades in Science because I can't dissect frogs or insects or worms."

"You can't?" asked Stanley Froghorn. "Well, no matter, you can't stay here . . . ribbit . . . . It's my job to protect this pond and every living creature in it. You'll have to leave here right now! Ribbit! Ribbit!"

"I'm sorry," replied Tina. "I didn't mean to hurt you or any

of the creatures in the pond. I'll find my way home somehow.''

Tina pulled herself to her feet and looked across the pretty green meadow. Just then she saw the rest of the Gang running toward her. They were wearing white laboratory coats, and they were carrying big nets and jars of smelly liquid.

''Come on, Tina. We have to go catch some frogs for Science class,'' cried Billy Boulder.

''Yeah, we have to catch a bunch of them so we can dissect them,'' shouted Jessica Jones.

''Mikie and I are going to put some in our pockets to scare the other kids,'' exclaimed Timmy Thomas.

''You can't do that!'' exclaimed Tina.

"Sure we can," said Mikie Murphy, opening his pocket. "You just shove them in there."

"No," cried Tina. "I mean, you just can't go and catch those poor little frogs."

"We have to," added Patty Peterson. "It's okay as long as we don't get our clothes dirty."

"No! It's not okay!" cried Tina. "You just can't catch those nice frogs and cut them up like that!"

"But we need to know what makes them live," added Becky Boulder. "I know it doesn't seem very nice, but if we don't know how the parts of their bodies work, we won't be able to help other frogs when they are sick."

The Gang ran to the pond. Stanley Froghorn was screaming at them. "Get away! Ribbit! Get away!" he shouted.

Billy caught one of the frogs. "Come here, Tina. Dissect this frog!" he shouted. "The teacher will give you an A if you do it right!"

Tina started crying over and over again, "I can't do it! I can't do it!"

Then Tina became aware of someone shaking her. "Tina, Tina, wake up," her mom said. "You're having a bad dream."

Tina shook her head and sat up in bed. "Oh, I was just dreaming," she sighed.

The next week seemed to drag by. Tina hated going to Science class. The class was supposed to dissect the frogs on Friday. Tina was thinking about telling her mom that she wasn't feeling well so she wouldn't have to go to school. She knew if she did that, her mom would take her to the doctor and the doctor would know there was nothing wrong with her. Tina decided she would just have to go to school and try her best.

At lunchtime Tina wasn't hungry. She just moved her food around on the tray with her fork the entire lunch period. The bell rang, and it was time for Science class to begin.

Tina was the last one to enter the classroom. As she walked in, the teacher was taking the frogs out of a big jar of smelly liquid. The class was putting on smocks and getting out the dissecting tools. Tina sat down in her seat.

"I don't think I can do this," Tina said to Billy who was sitting at the table beside her.

"Look, Tina, if you can't do it, then don't do it," replied Billy.

"The teacher said I had to if I wanted to get an A," cried Tina. "I have to make an A! I just have to!"

But Tina couldn't do it. The frog she was to work on lay in front of her. "I wonder if you're one of Mr. Froghorn's friends," she thought to herself. "I wonder if Stanley Froghorn himself is laying on one of these tables."

"Where do these frogs come from?" Tina asked the teacher. "Do people go out to ponds and catch them in nets, or what?"

"No, Tina," assured the teacher. "These frogs are raised especially for Science classes like this one. Top scientists even use these frogs to study. By studying frogs like these, our medical doctors learn how to help people when they are sick or need an operation. These frogs really help people by giving up their lives so we can study them."

Tina stared down at the frog. She tried and tried, but she still couldn't convince herself that she should cut up this frog.

Science class seemed to last forever that day. Finally, the bell rang. Tina took her undissected frog up to the teacher. "I'm sorry," she said. "But I couldn't do it. I'll just have to take a lower grade."

Tina did get a grade which was lower than she would have liked to get. "What did you get in Science?" asked Patty Peterson. "I got an A."

"I got a C," sighed Tina. "What am I going to do? I can't show this to my mom."

"Tina, a C isn't so bad," said Becky Boulder. "C is average. It's not like you got an F or anything."

"Yeah, but I've never gotten a C before," cried Tina. "I'm really going to be in trouble when Mom sees this."

Tina was scared. She didn't want to show her report card to her mom. She just knew her mom would be mad at her for getting a C.

When Tina got home, she stopped on her porch before going into the house. "I just can't take this report card in for my mom to see," she thought to herself. "I know, I'll just hide it in the bushes."

Tina stuck the report card deep down into the bush beside her front door, way down where no one could see it.

The next morning, on the way to school, Jessica Jones asked Tina, "What did your mom say about the C you got in Science?"

"She didn't say anything," replied Tina. "I didn't show it to her."

"You didn't?" asked Billy Boulder. "How could you not show it to her?"

"Didn't she see your report card when you came home from school?" asked Sherry Summers.

"I didn't take it in the house," sighed Tina. "I hid it in the bushes by the front door."

"Tina, your mom has to sign it before you can bring it back to school," reminded Mikie Murphy.

"I know," replied Tina. "Maybe I could just tell the teacher that I lost it. I did, kind of, didn't I?"

"I don't think you could say hiding it in the bushes is losing it," remarked Patty Peterson. "Besides, the teacher would just give you another one."

"If you think your mom is going to be mad about your getting a C, just wait until she finds out you didn't show her your report card," said Timmy Thomas.

"Yeah, she's really going to be mad about that," added Andy Andrews.

Tina worried about her report card all day. "What if it falls out of the bush and Mom finds it," she thought. "I'll check when I get home and make sure it's still there."

Tina did check when she got home from school that day. The report card was still there. "Maybe I'll show it to her in the morning," she thought. "I'll just leave it here in the bush for tonight."

After Tina went to bed that night, she heard thunder way off in the distance. "Oh, I hope it doesn't rain," she thought. "I hope the wind doesn't blow hard and blow the report card out of the bush."

Tina lay there listening as the thunder got closer and closer. The wind started blowing harder and harder. It whistled past her window as if it were saying to her, "If you don't show it to her, I will."

Tina didn't sleep all night long. As soon as the rain stopped and it was daylight, Tina ran out the front door. Her mom had gone to get some milk for breakfast. "Please, be here," she cried as she scrambled through the bush. But the report card wasn't there. "Oh, no!" cried Tina. "Did Mom find it? Did it blow away? Where is it, anyway?"

Tina saw her mom's car turn the corner. She ran back inside. "Oh, I hope she didn't find it," she thought.

All through breakfast, Tina's mom didn't say a word about the report card.

As Tina left the house to go to school, she wanted to look for the report card again, but she couldn't. Today, her mom watched from the front door as Tina started down the street. "I know she found it," thought Tina. "She never stands at the door when I leave for school. I wonder why she didn't say anything about it?"

Patty Peterson came running up behind Tina. "Tina, Tina, look what I found in my front yard," she called as she waved the report card back and forth in the air.

"My report card!" exclaimed Tina. "How did it get in your yard?"

"I guess the storm last night blew it out of the bush and into my yard," replied Patty. "Tina, haven't you shown it to your mom yet?"

"No, I haven't," sighed Tina. "I just don't want to get into trouble over a C on my report card."

"Tina, we were supposed to bring them back to school today," said Becky Boulder.

"And signed by our parents," added Jessica Jones.

REPORT CARD
TINA
REPORT CARD

When they got to school, the teacher asked for the report cards to be placed on his desk. "I forgot mine," said Tina. "I mean, I lost mine."

"Well, which is it?" asked the teacher. "You forgot it, or you lost it?"

"Well, I didn't exactly lose it," sighed Tina. "I just haven't had my mom sign it yet, but I will tonight. I'll bring it tomorrow."

"All right," said the teacher. "But see that you do."

Tina walked home from school very slowly that day. She thought and thought about what she should do. She stopped at

Jessica Jones' house to talk to Jessica. "I don't want to get into trouble over a dumb C on my report card," she said. "I've always gotten straight A's, and Mom has always said how proud she is of me. She's going to be so disappointed."

"Maybe she won't be too mad," assured Jessica.

"I hope you're right," sighed Tina.

When Tina walked in the front door, her mom met her. "Tina, is there something you want to talk to me about?" she asked.

"What do you mean, Mom?" asked Tina.

"Your teacher called today," added Mrs. Tansell. "It seems that you got your report card on Monday and didn't tell me about it. Why didn't you show it to me, Tina?"

"Because I was afraid you would get mad at me," sighed Tina. "I got a C in Science, and I figured I would get in trouble if you saw it."

"Did you try to do your best in Science?" asked Mrs. Tansell.

"Yes, Mom, I did," cried Tina. "I just couldn't cut up those frogs and yukky insects and worms."

"All I've ever wanted you to do is your best," said Mrs. Tansell. "If you did your best, then that's all you can do. You can't get A's all the time."

"You mean you're not mad? You still love me?" asked Tina.

"Of course, I still love you," replied Mrs. Tansell. "I can understand that cutting up those frogs and insects might not be something you would like to do. I just hope the next time you have a problem you will talk to me about it. No matter how big or small your problems are, I'm here to help you."

Tina went to her room and plopped down on the bed. She picked up her big stuffed frog doll. "That's funny," she said to the frog. "You look just like Stanley Froghorn. Just think, all the worrying I've done for nothing. I should have shown that report card to Mom in the first place. In fact, I should have talked to her about the dissecting when I started having trouble with it. From now on, I'll know that if I've done my best, that's all I can do. I'll know that I don't have to be perfect at everything. I just have to be honest."